Copyright © 2020 by The Fartist

All rights reserved. This book or any portion thereof may not be reproduced or used in any manner whatsoever without the express written permission of the publisher except for the use of brief quotations in a book review.

Printed in the United States of America

First Printing, 2020

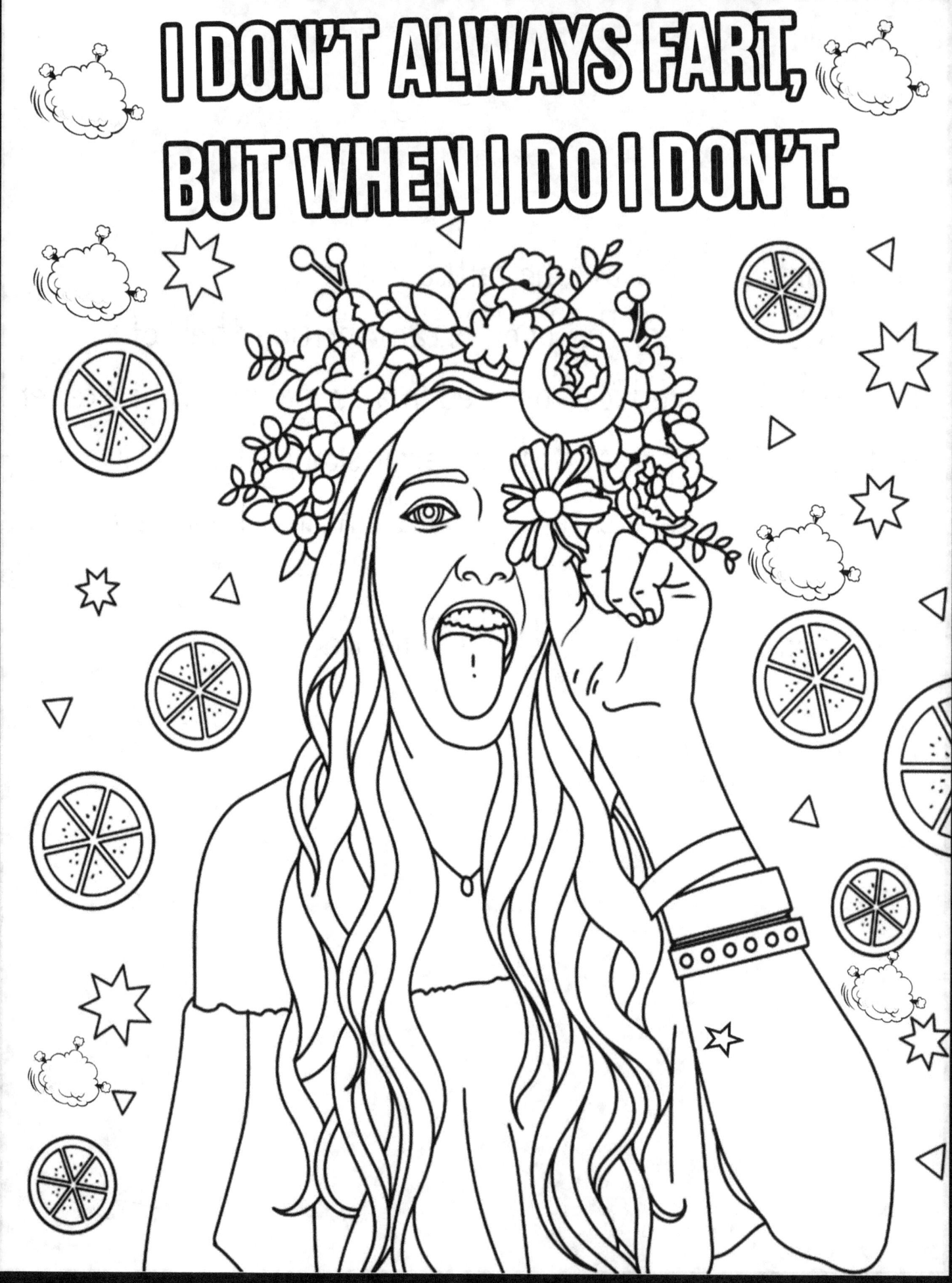

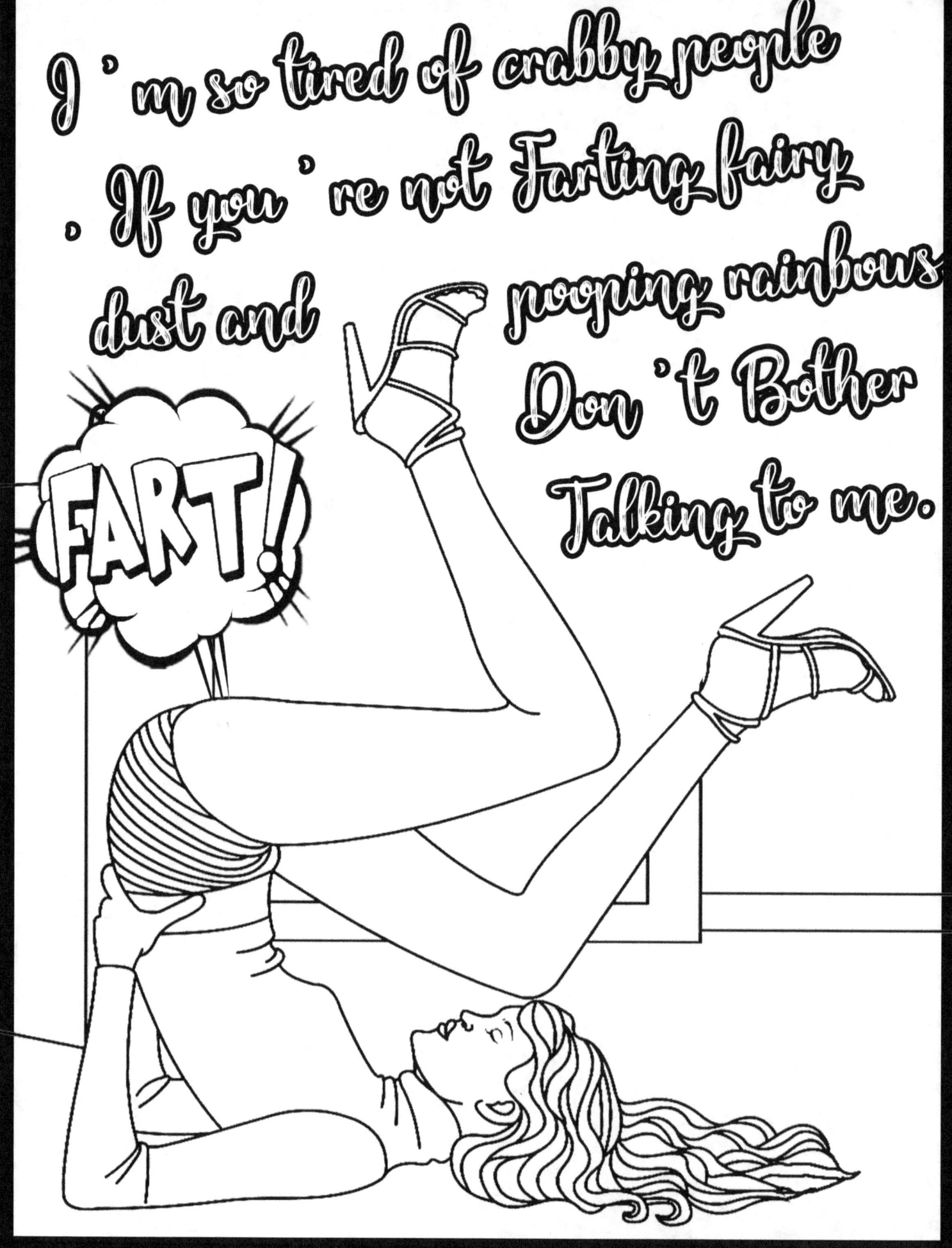

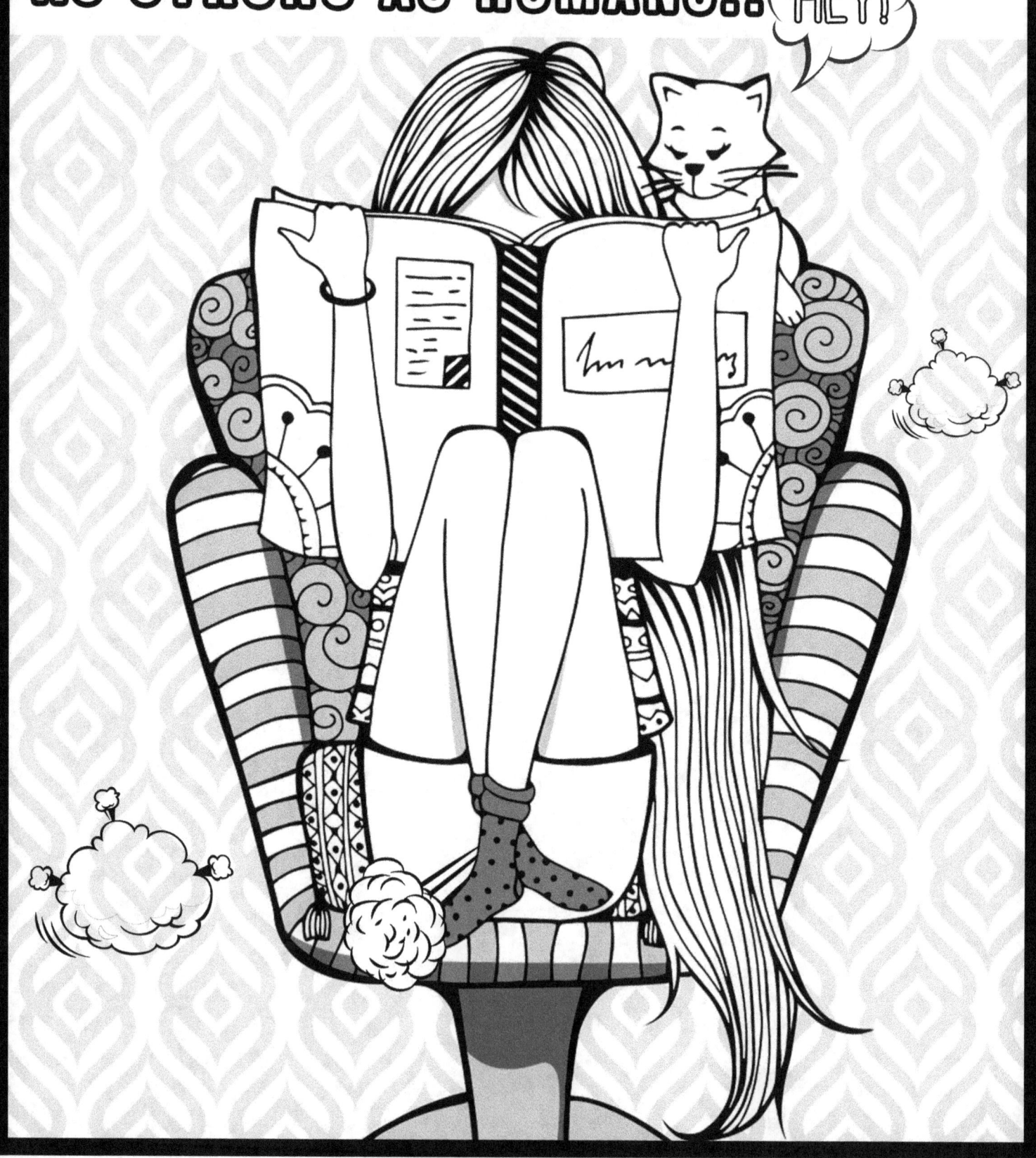

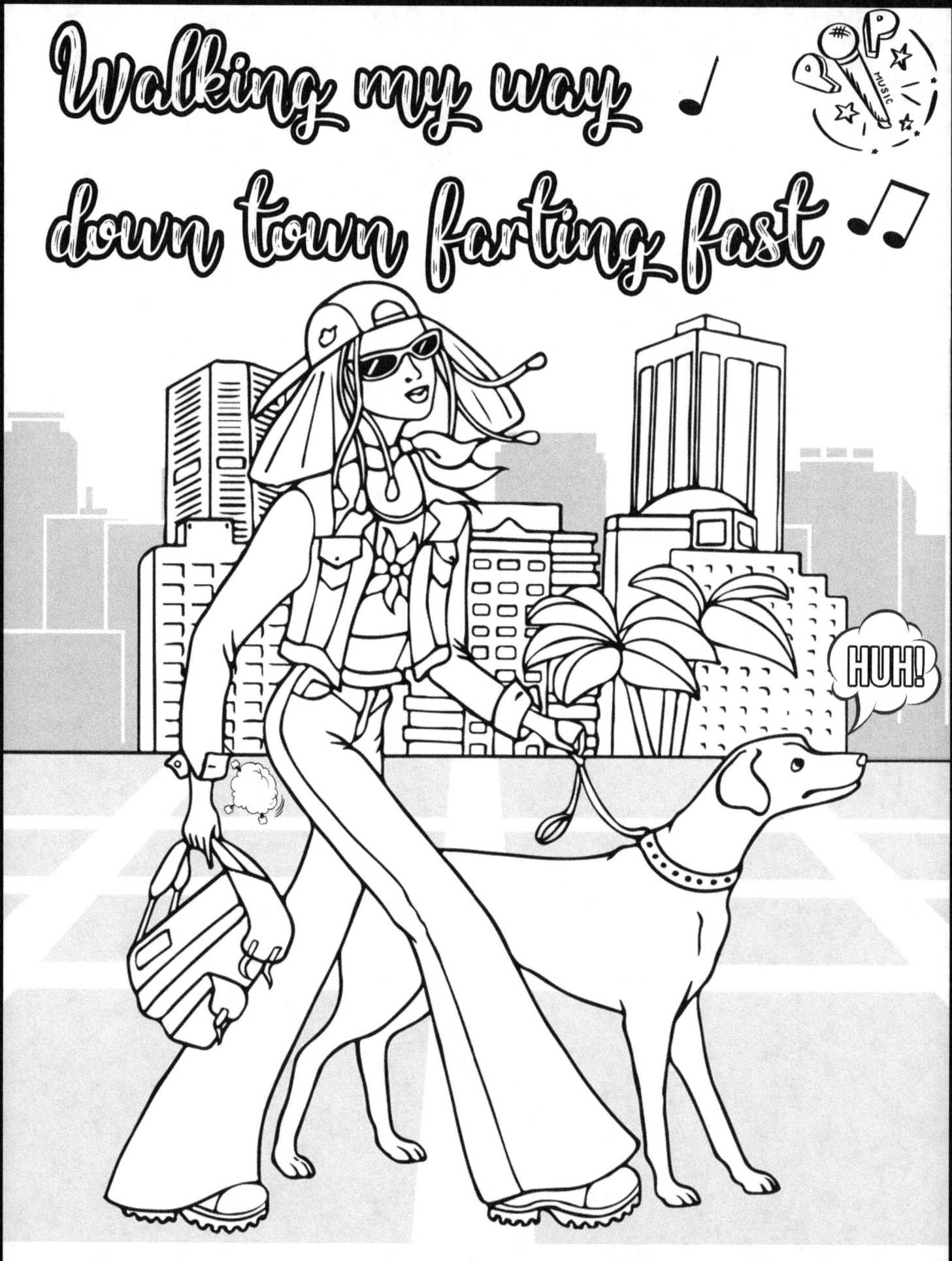

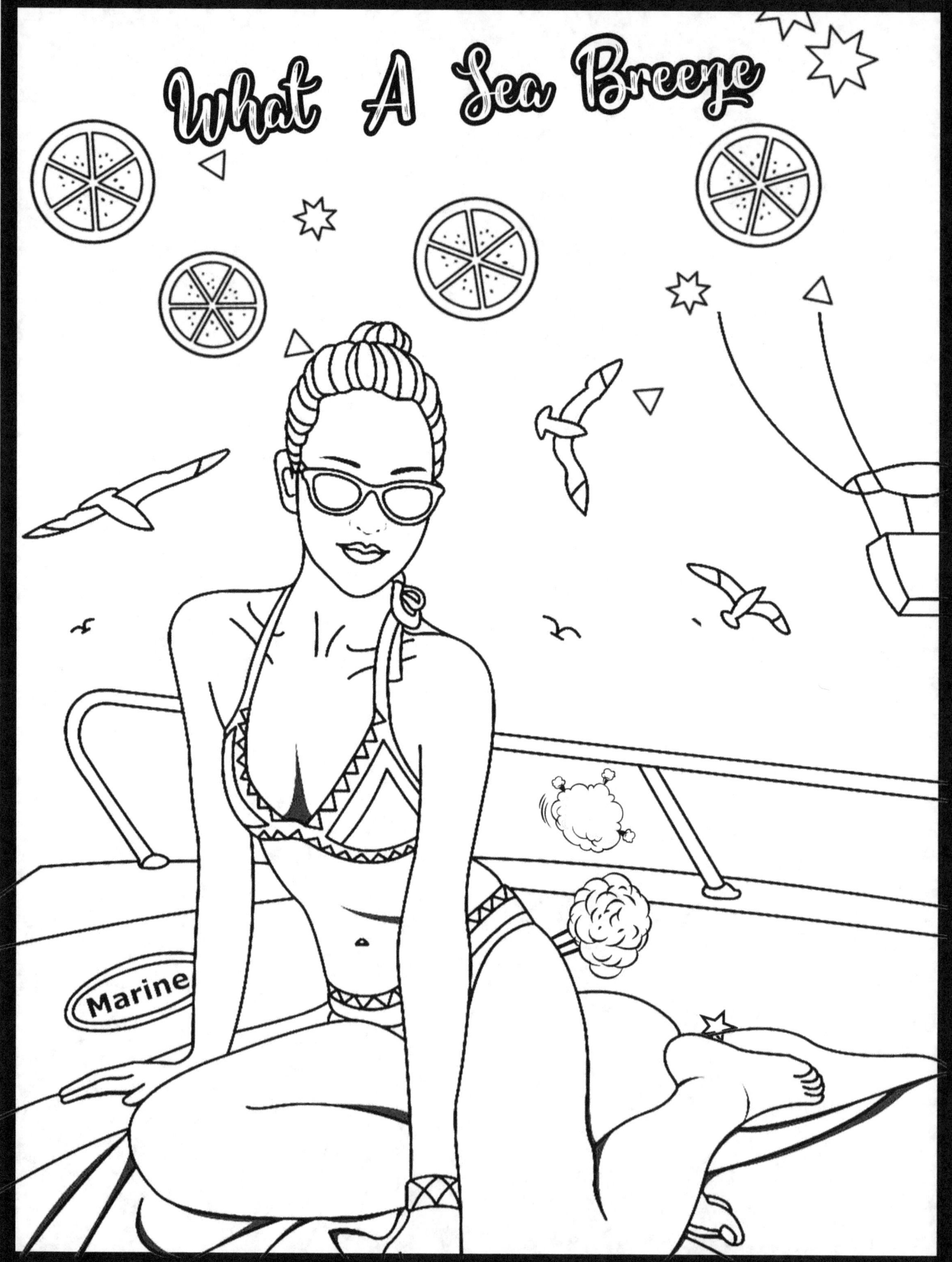

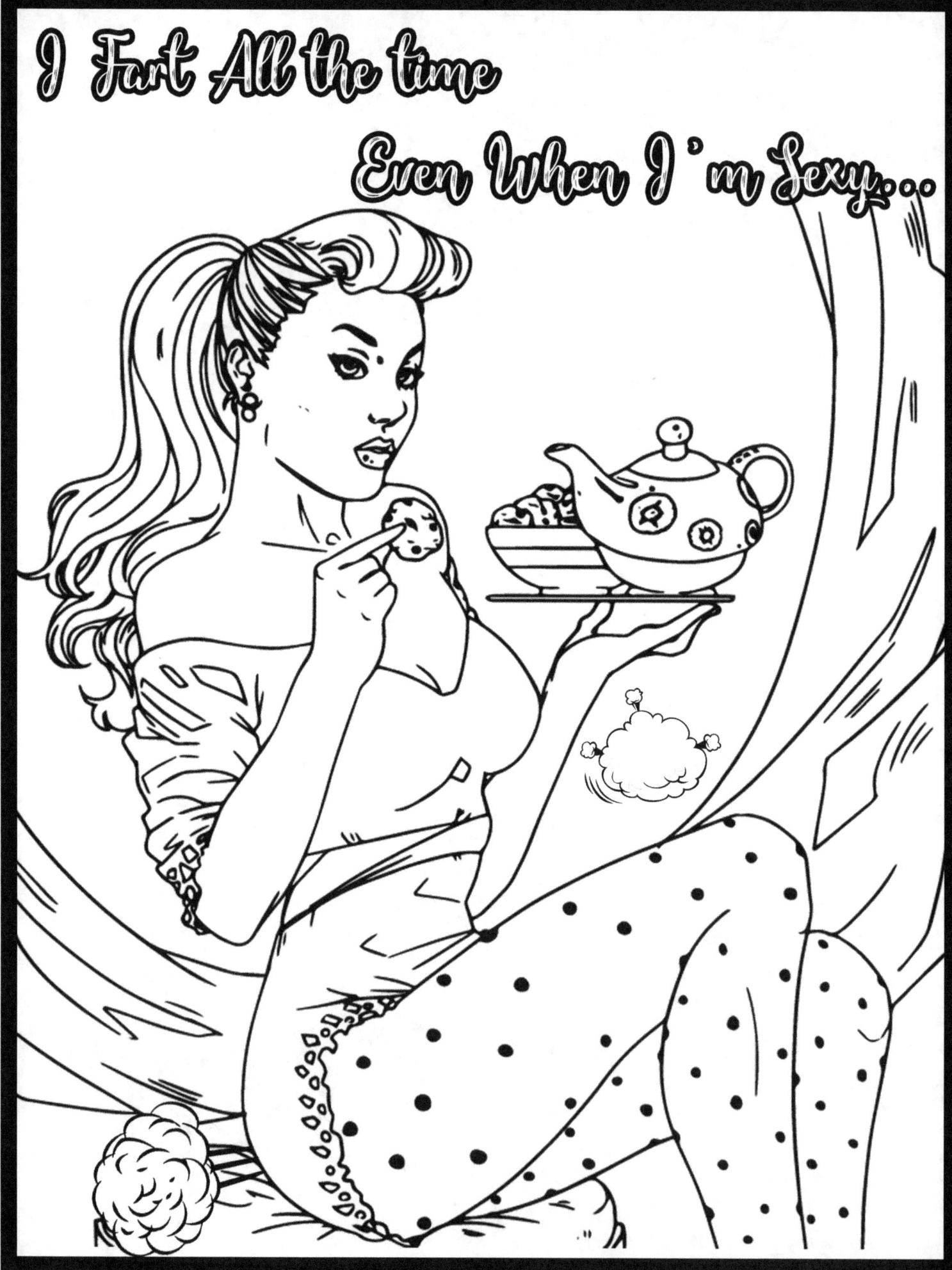

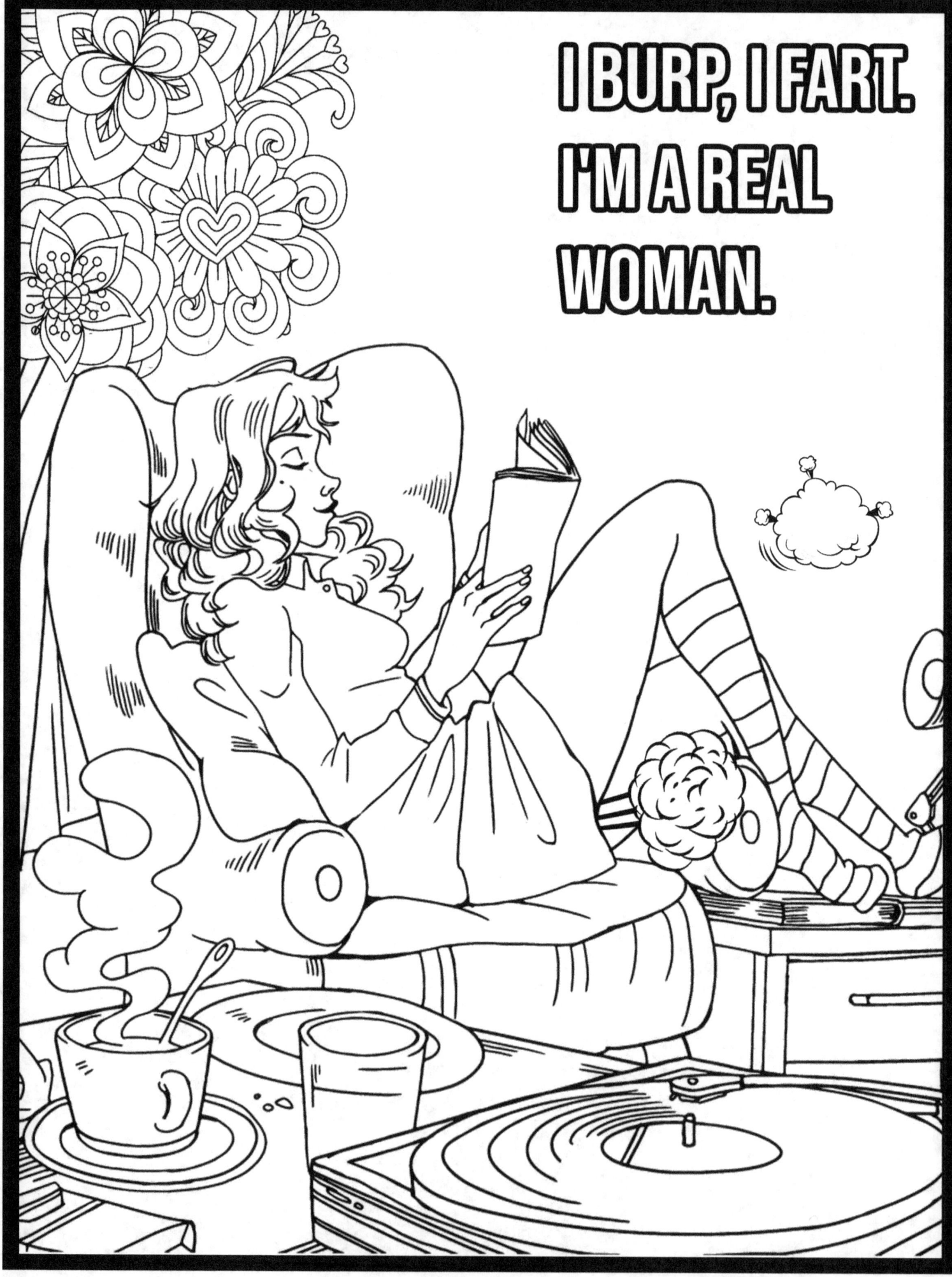

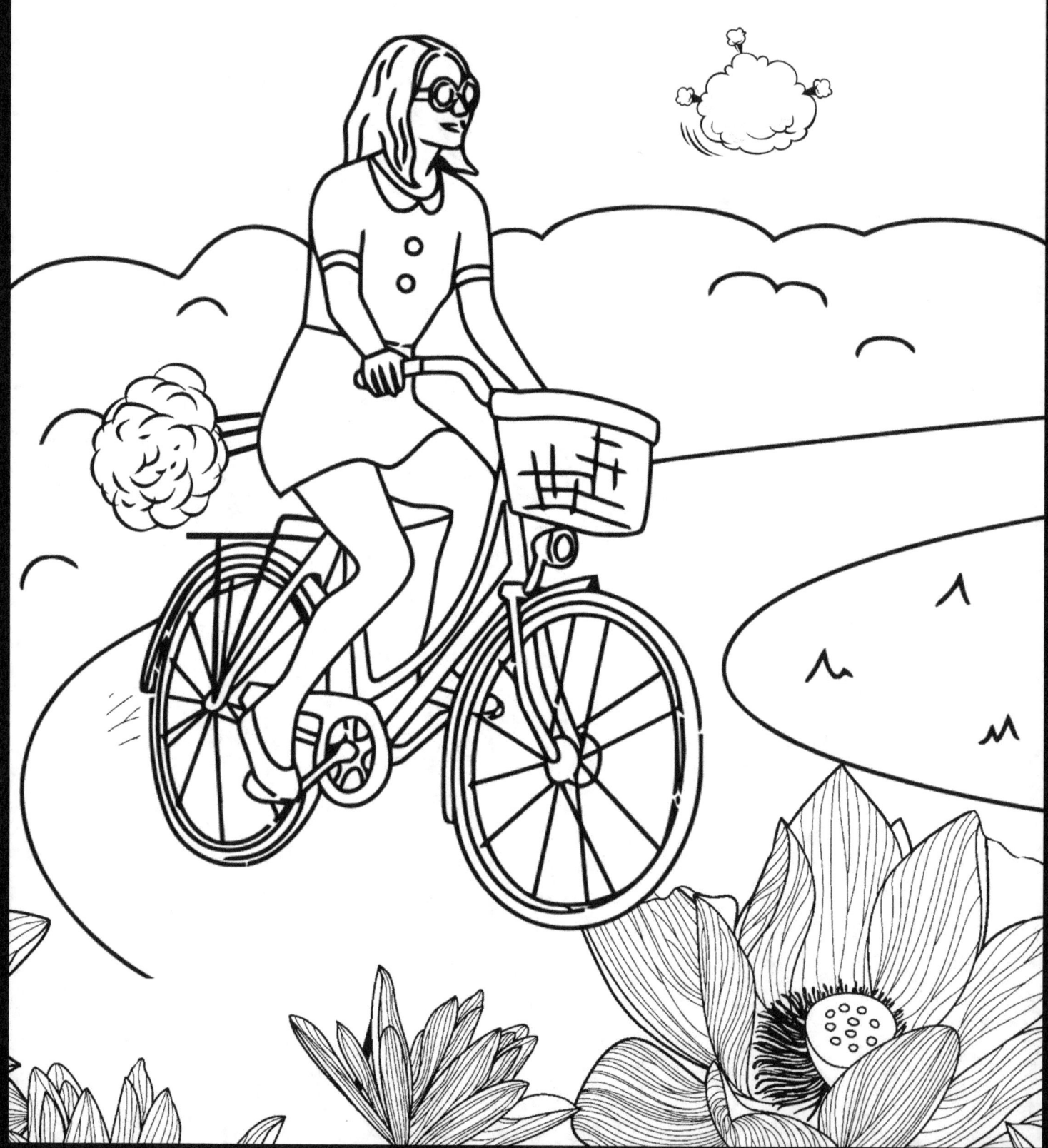

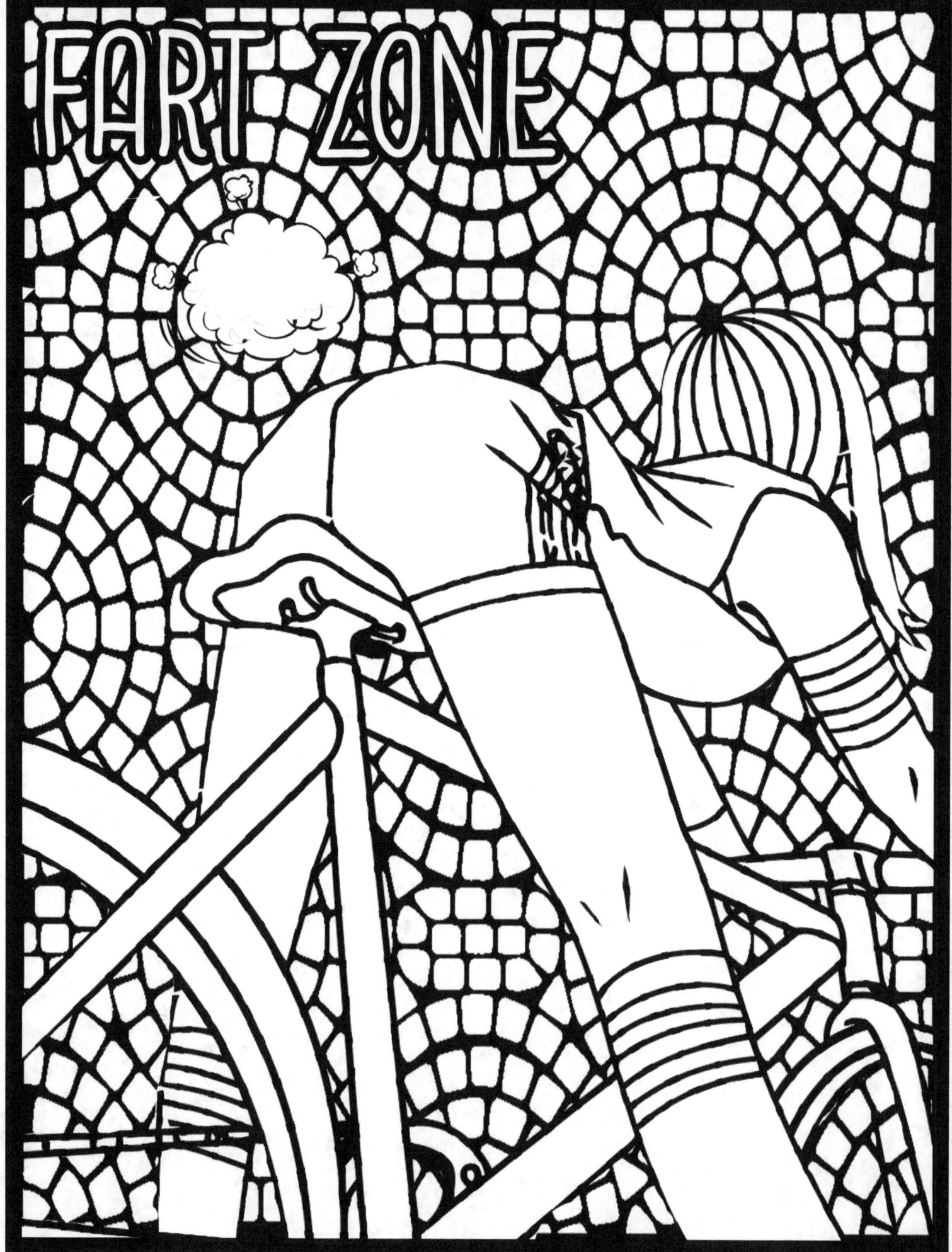

Easter Farts

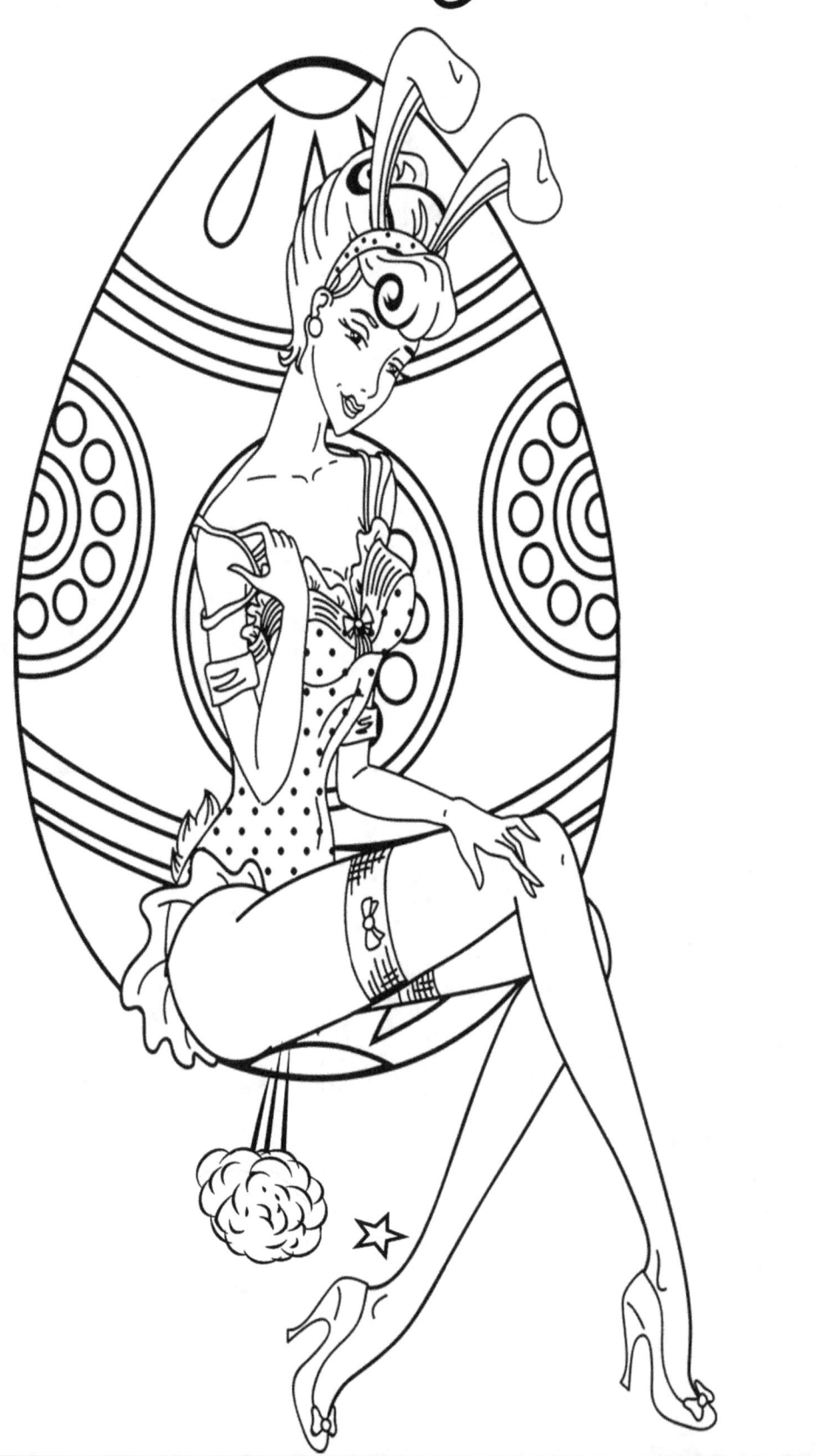

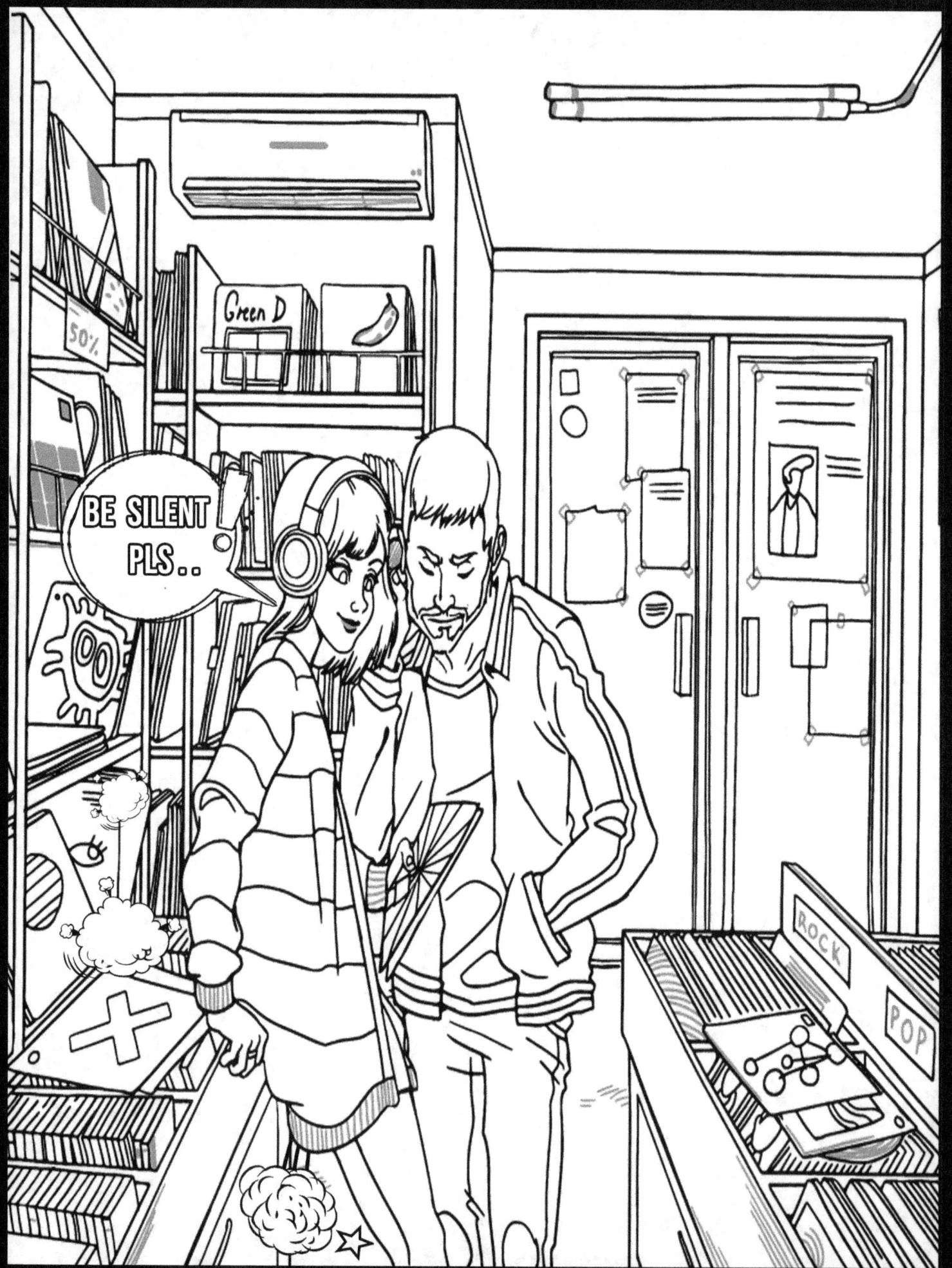

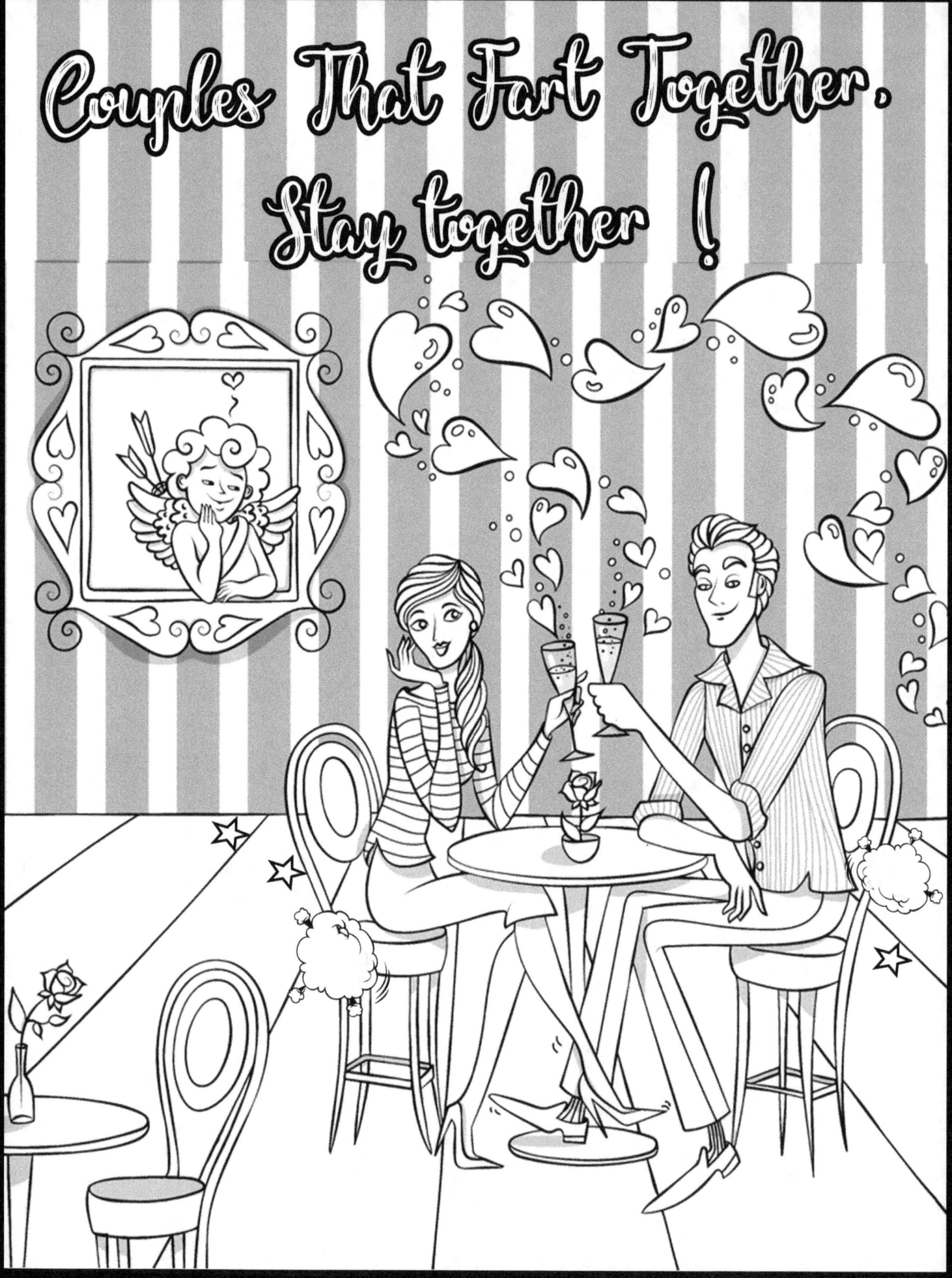

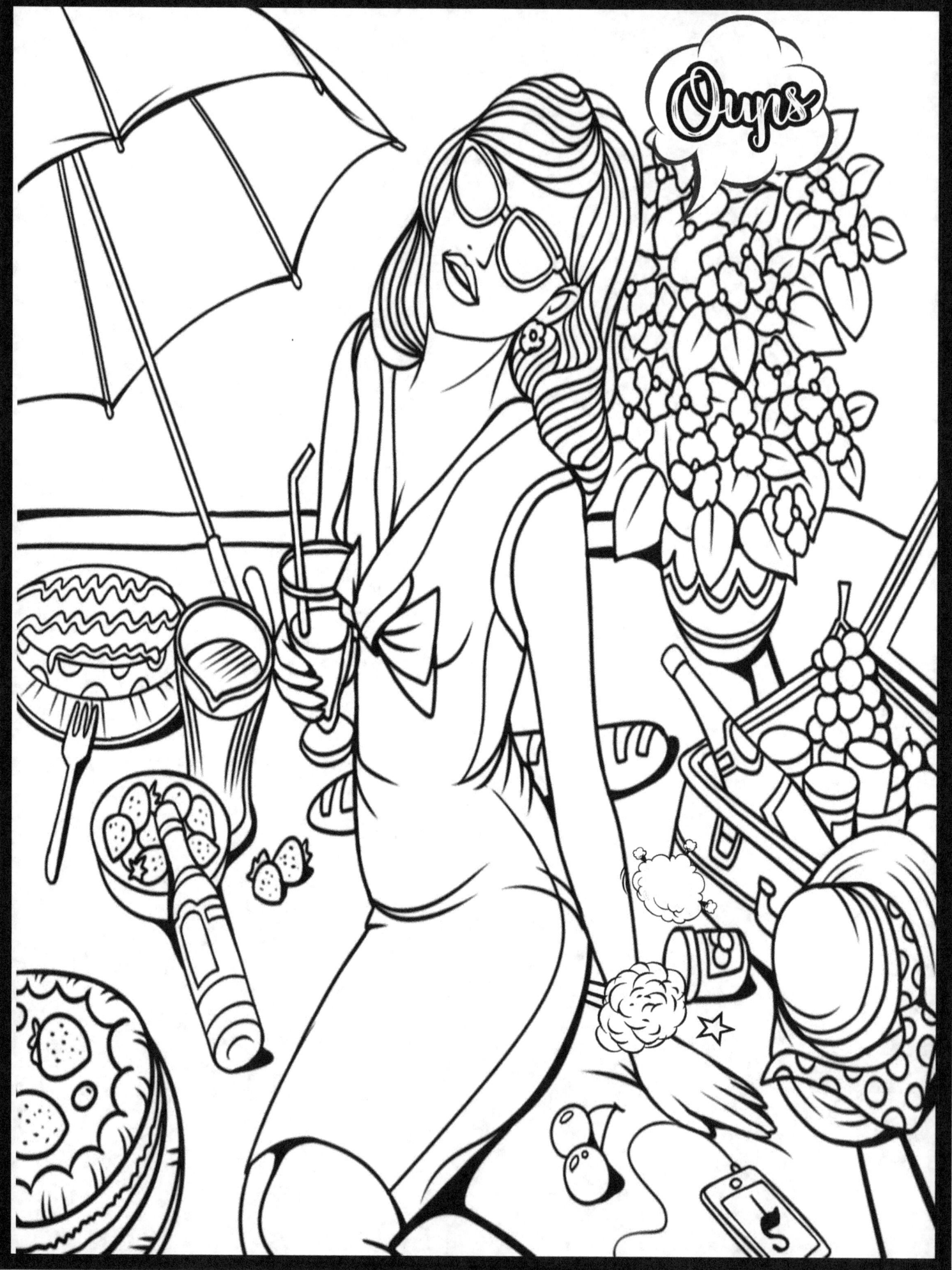

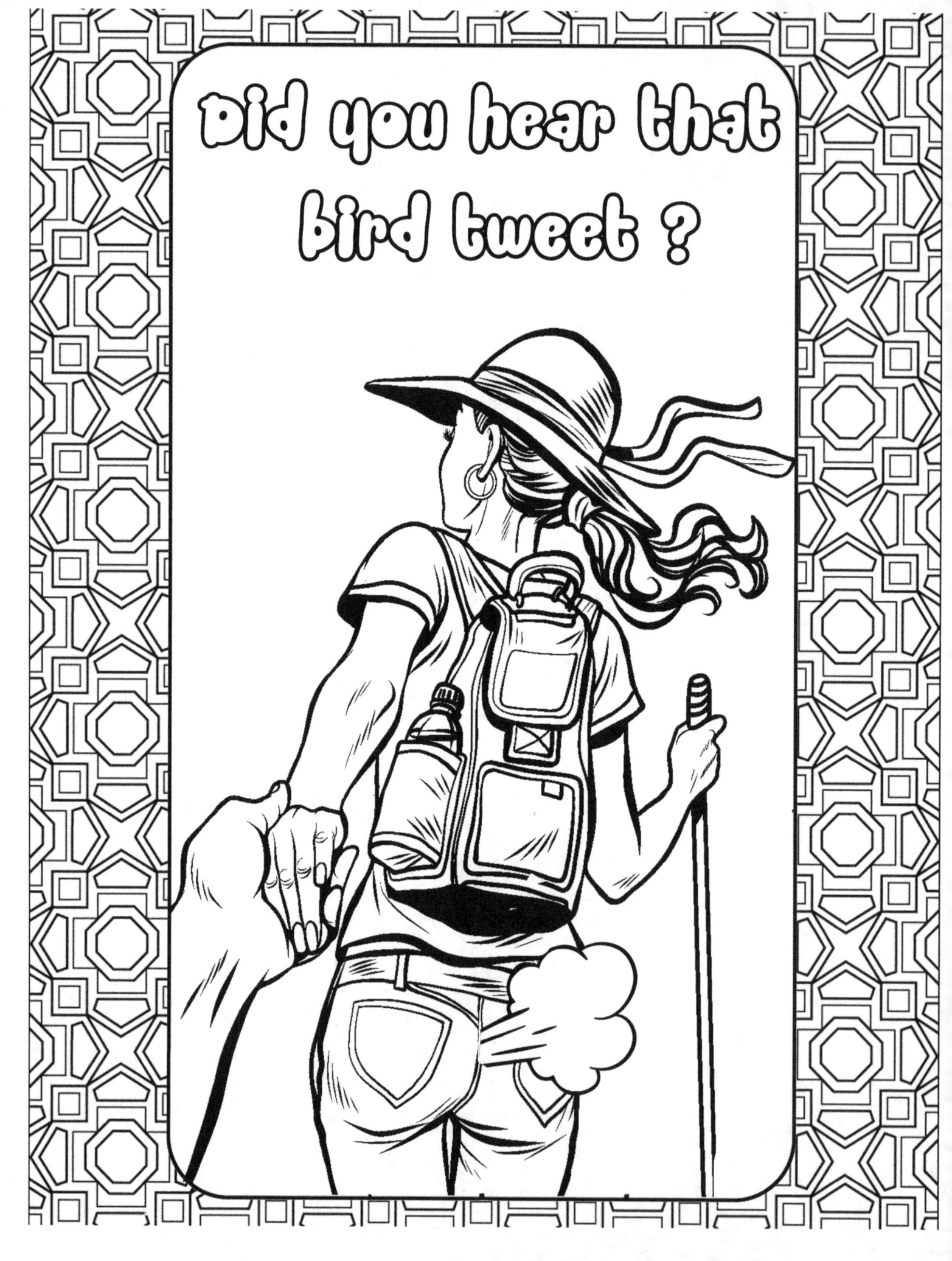

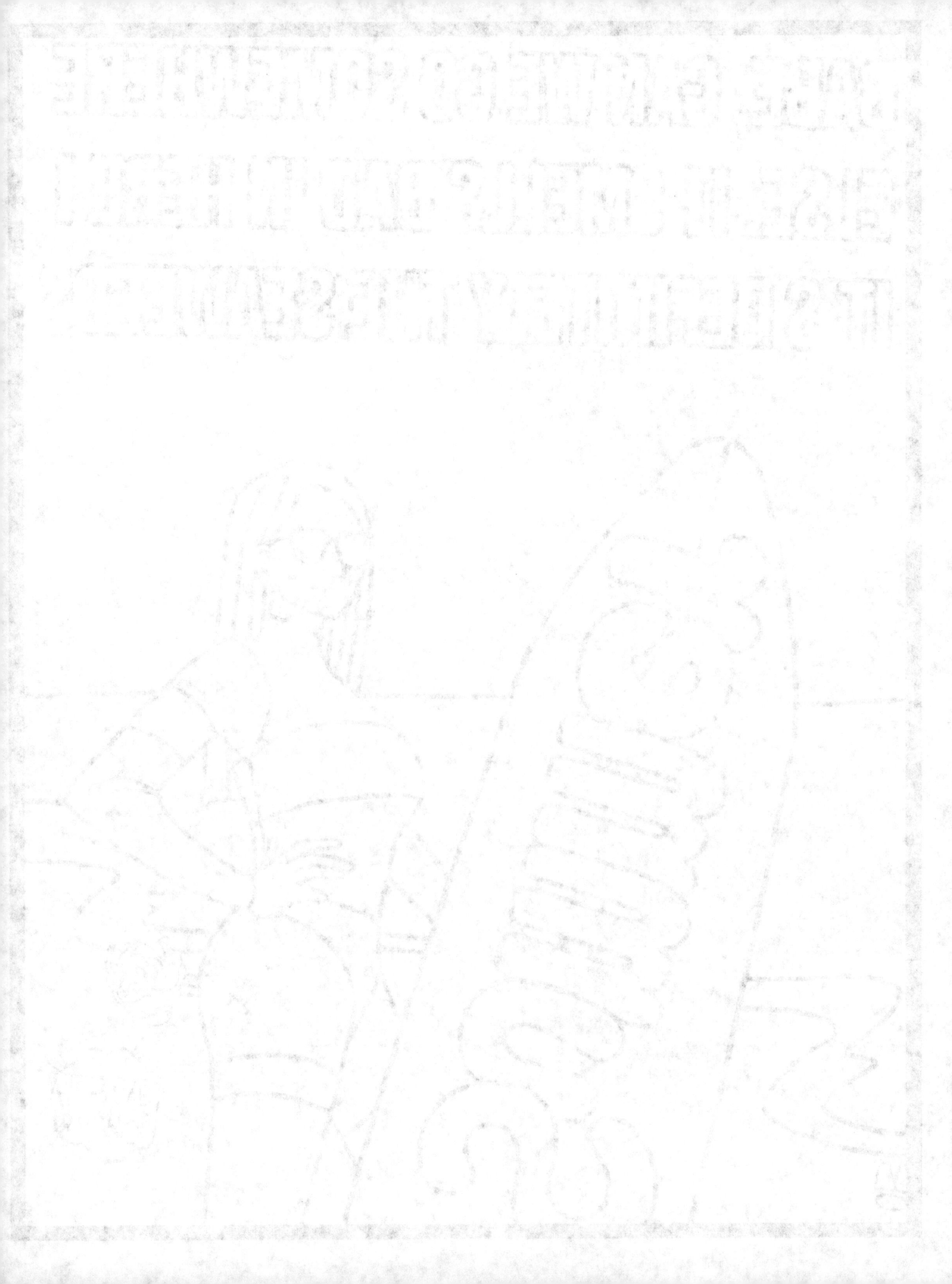

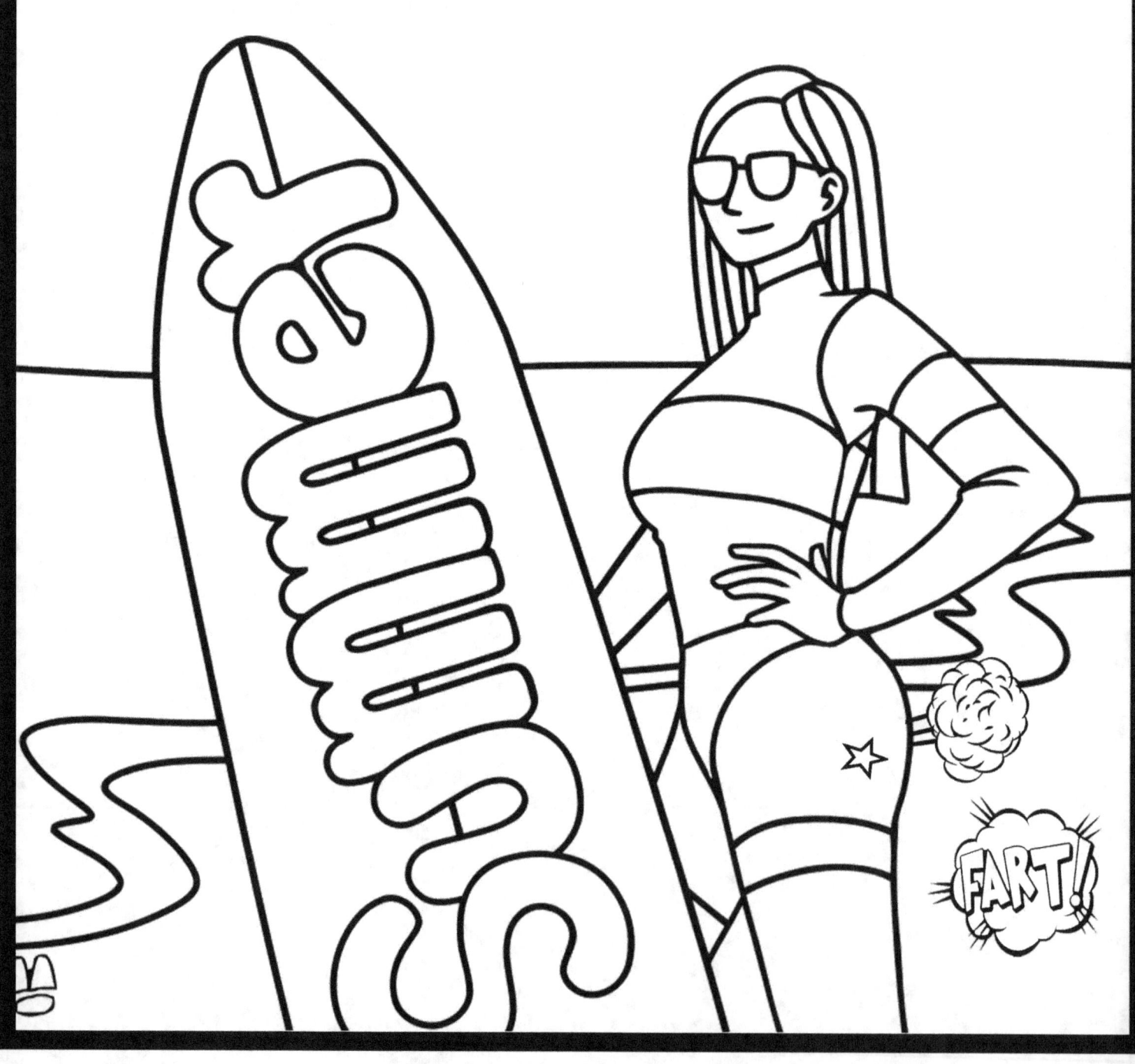

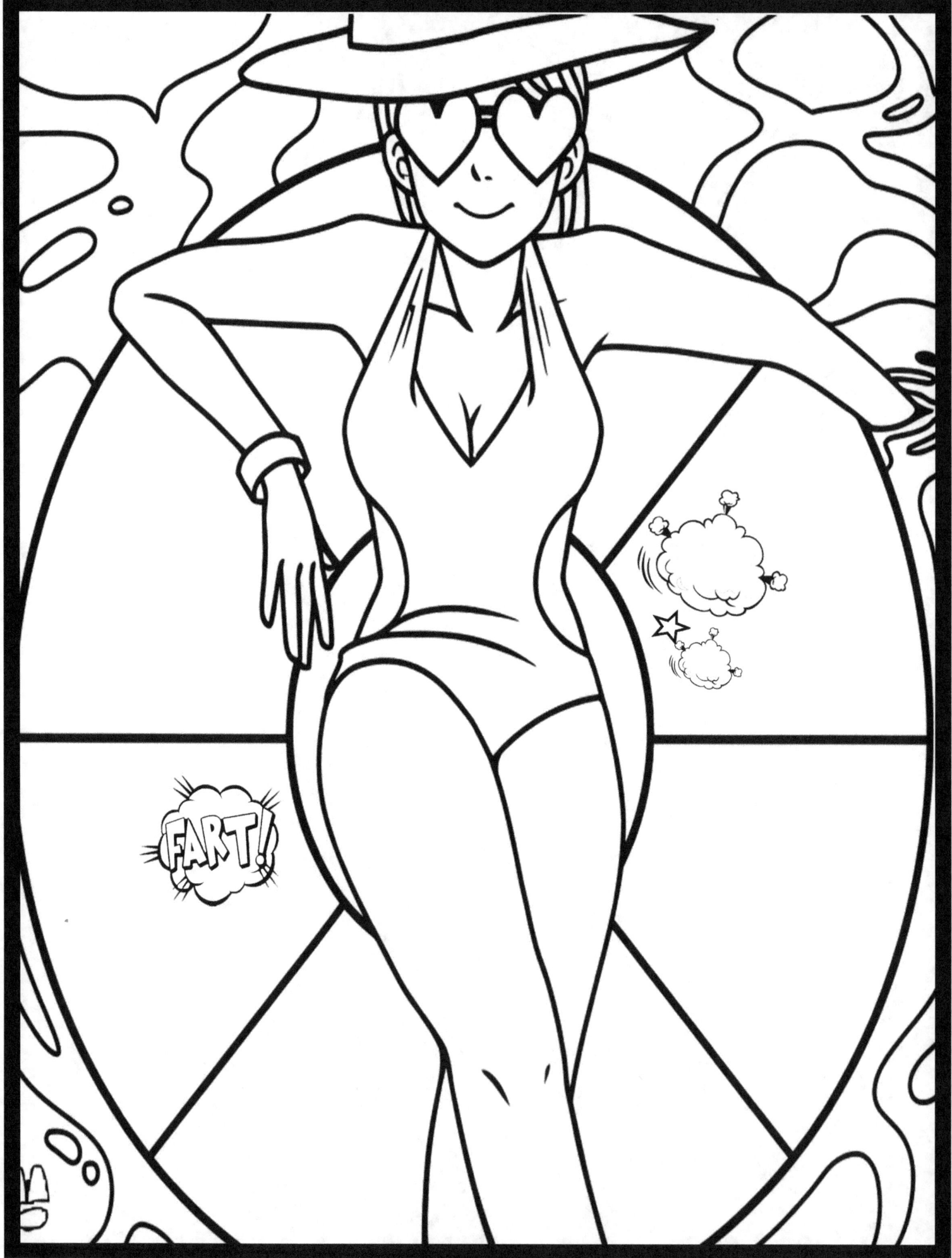

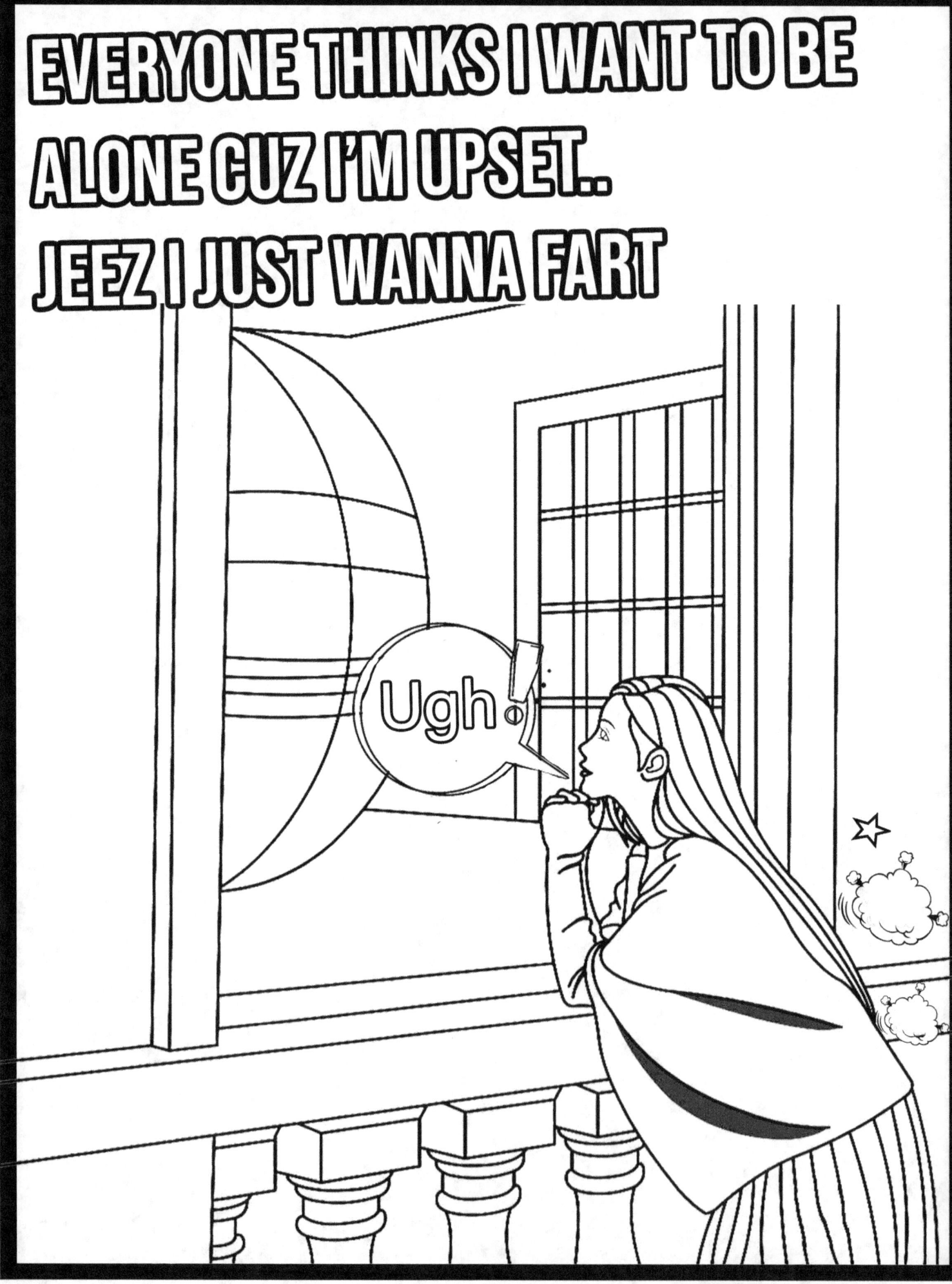

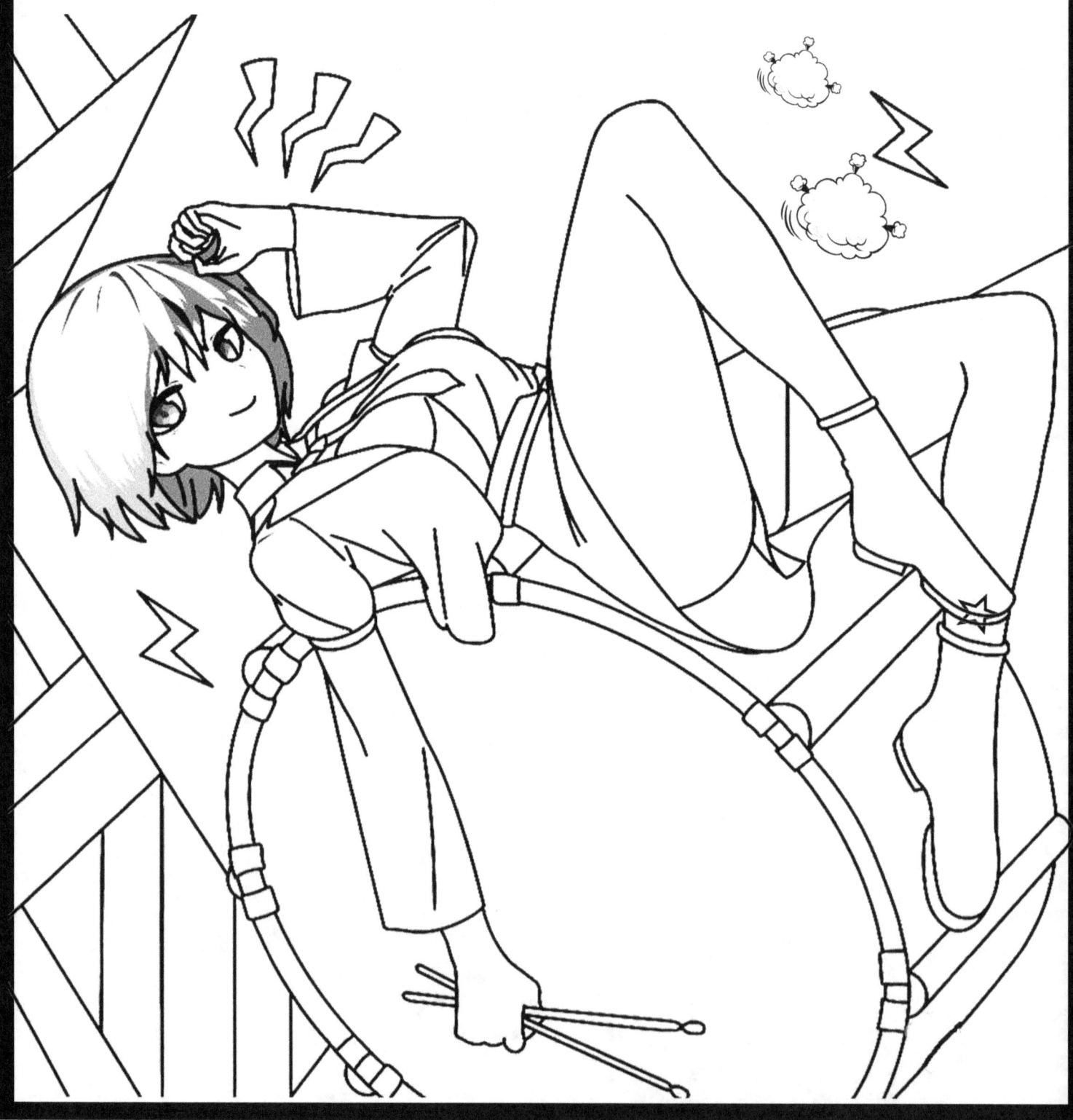

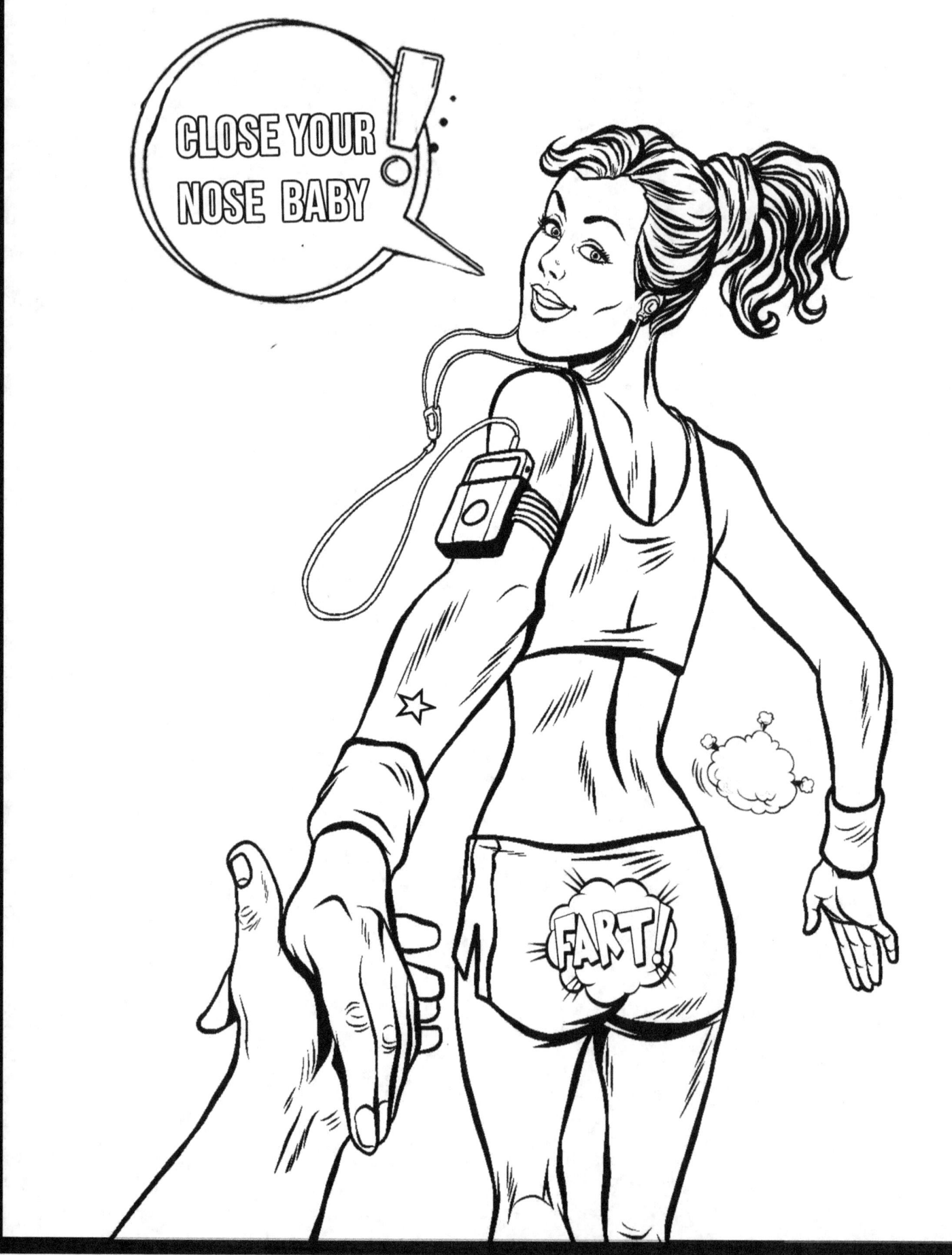

The Fairy Fart

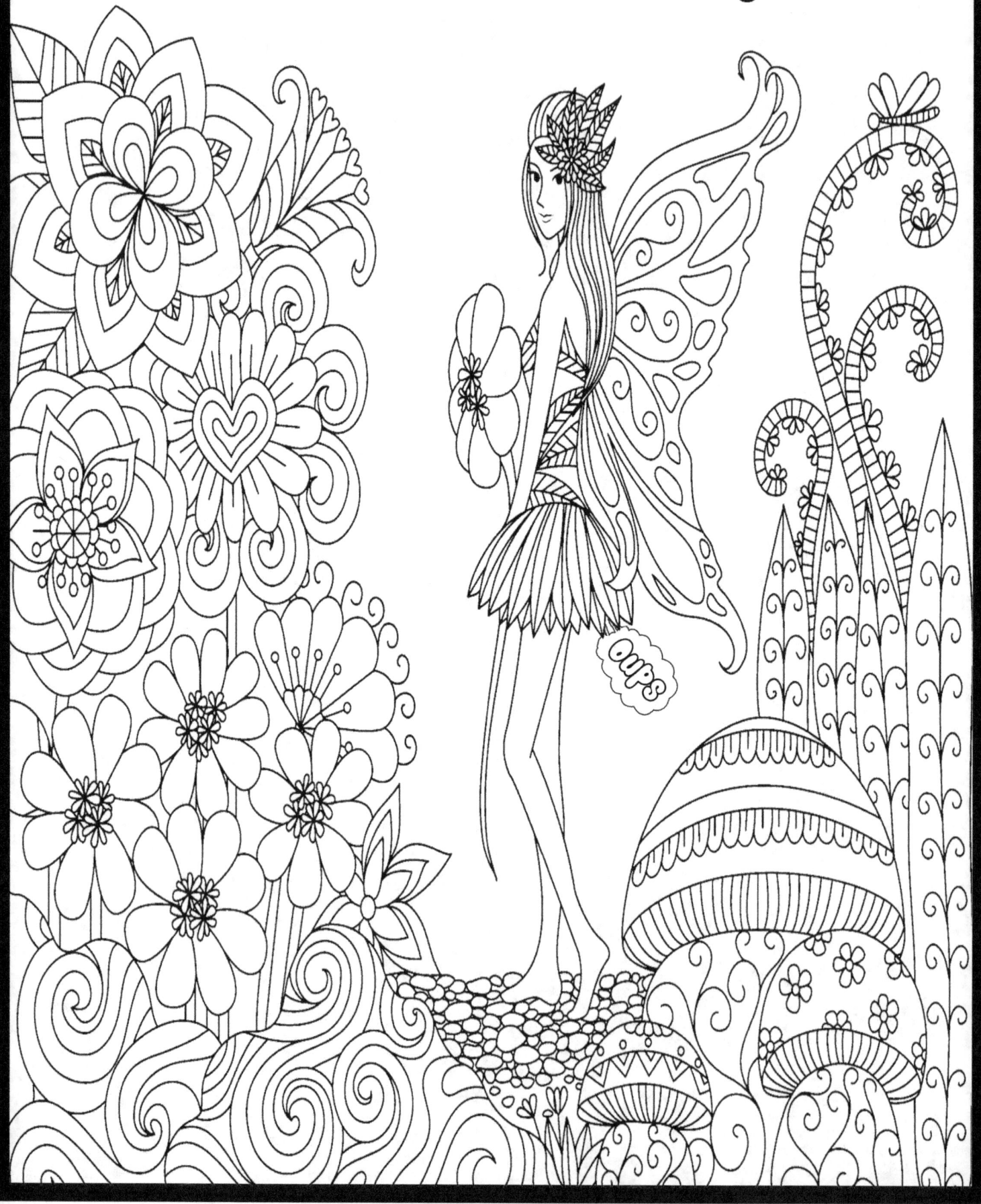

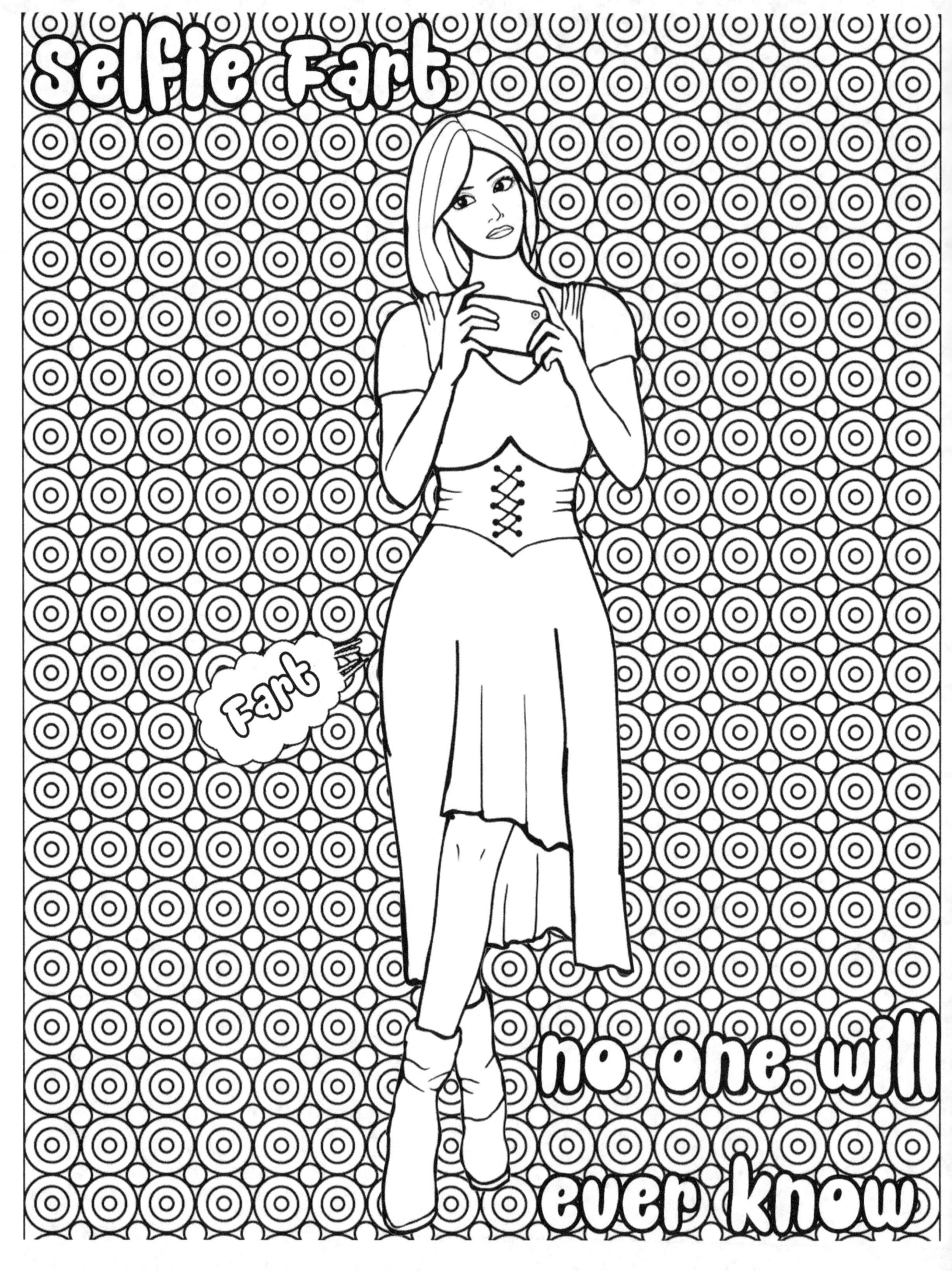

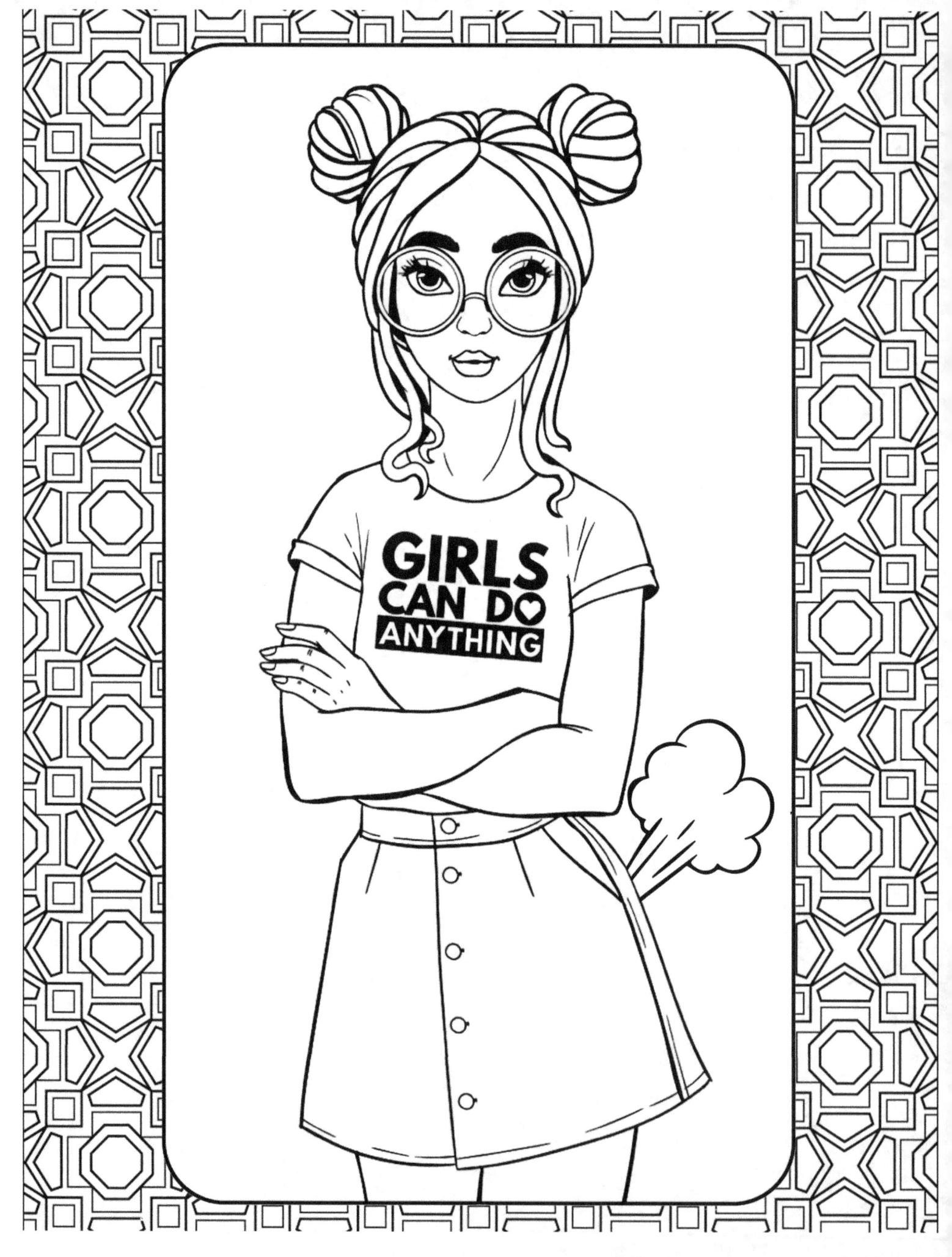

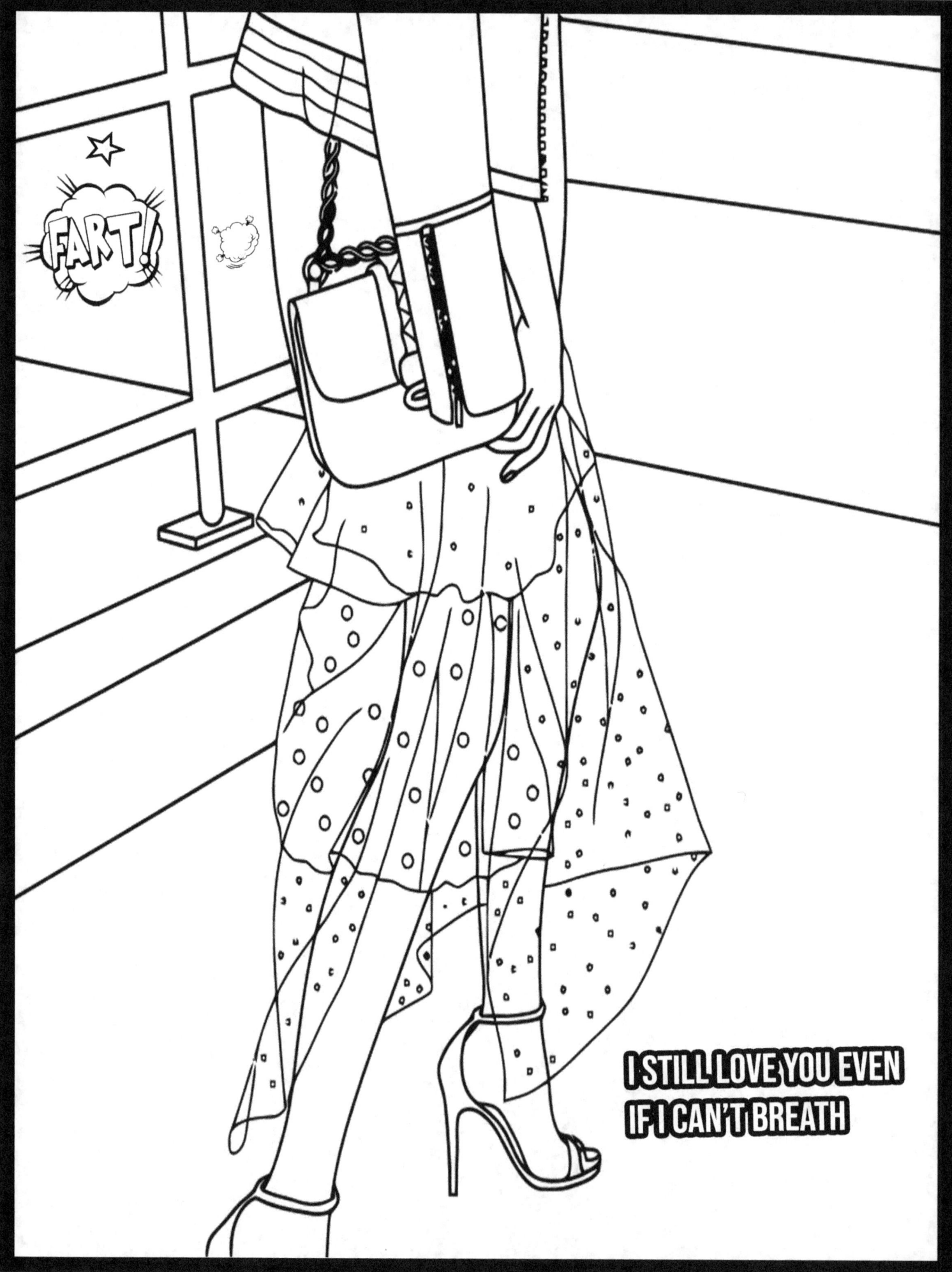

DO YOU SMELL THAT ?

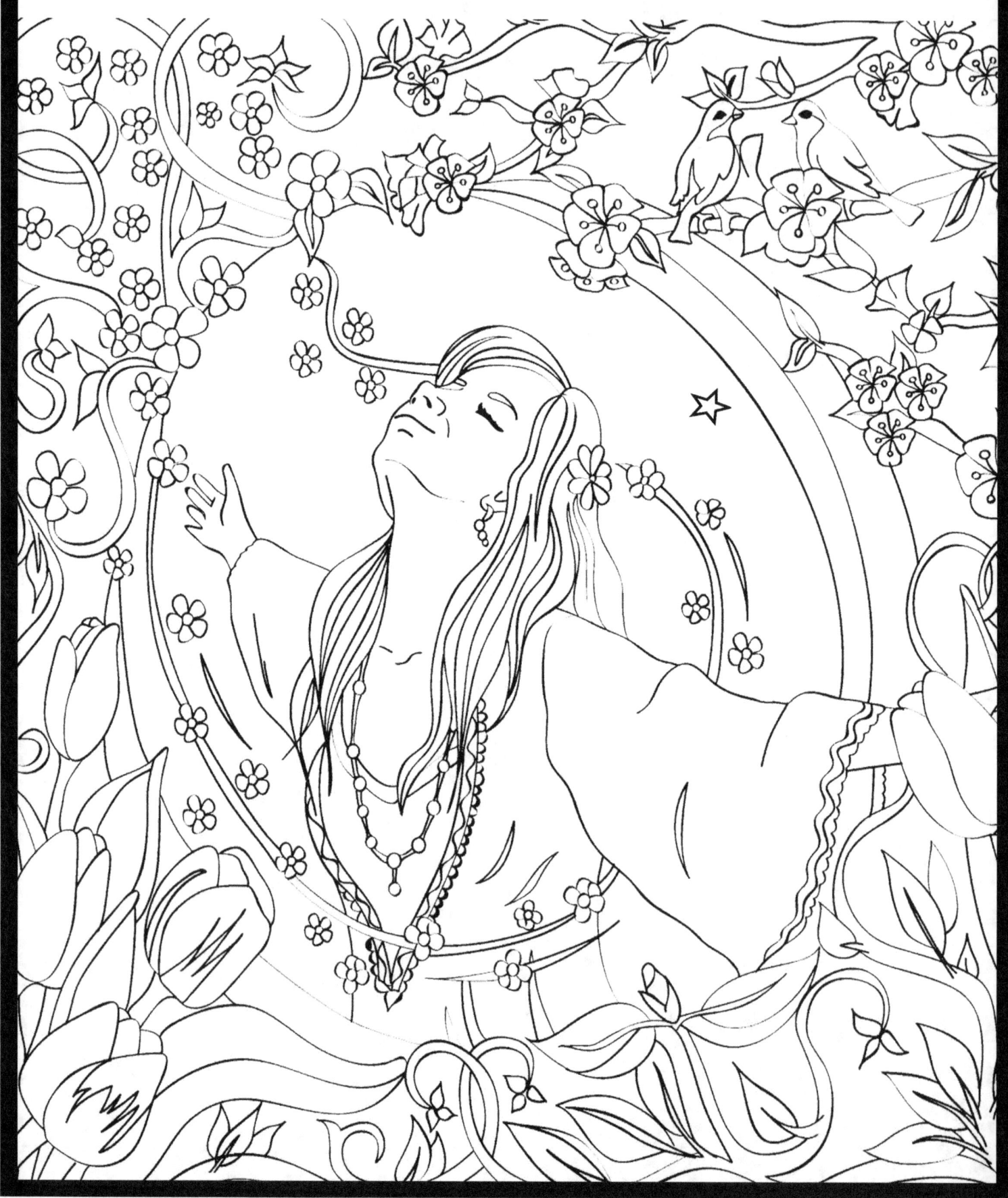

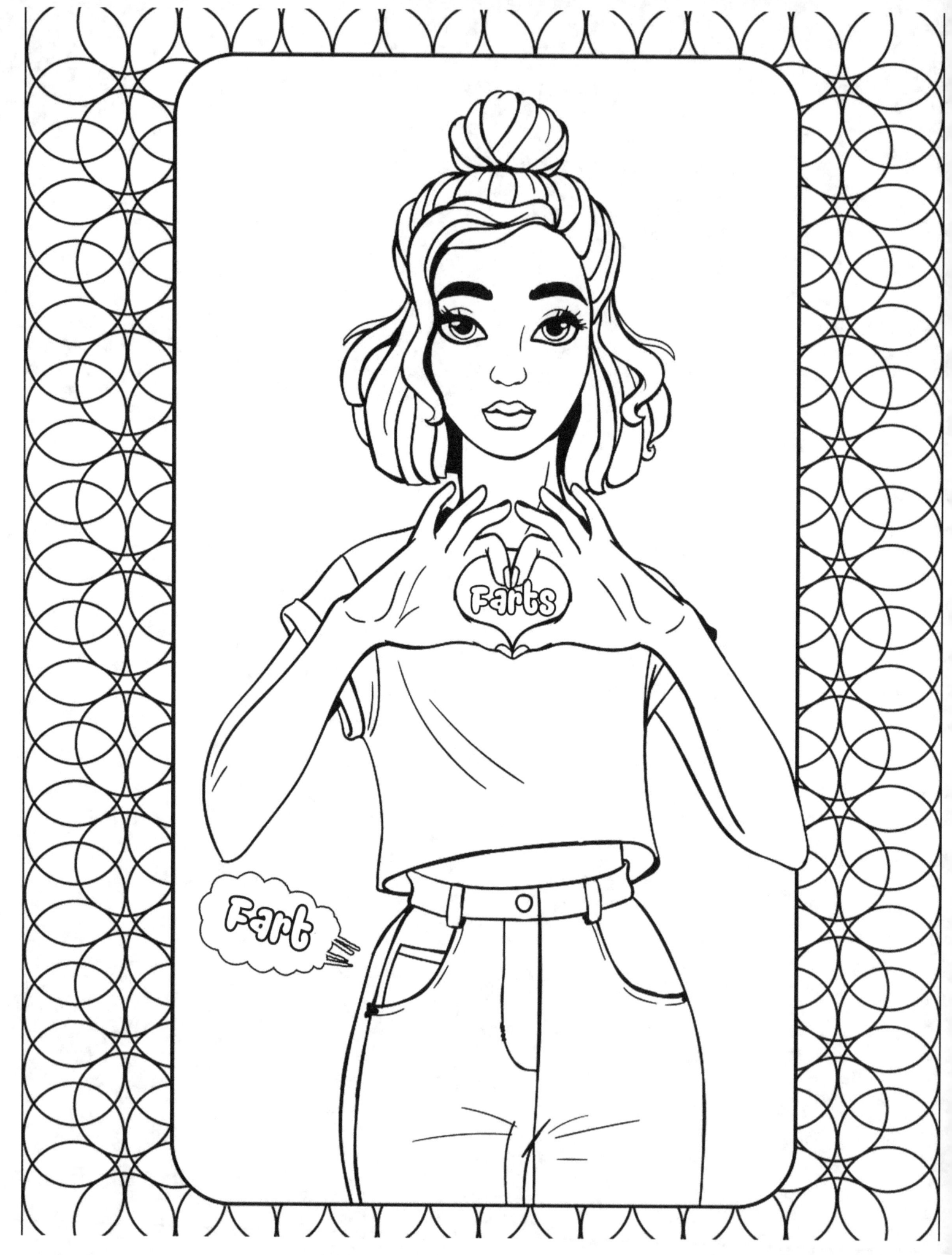

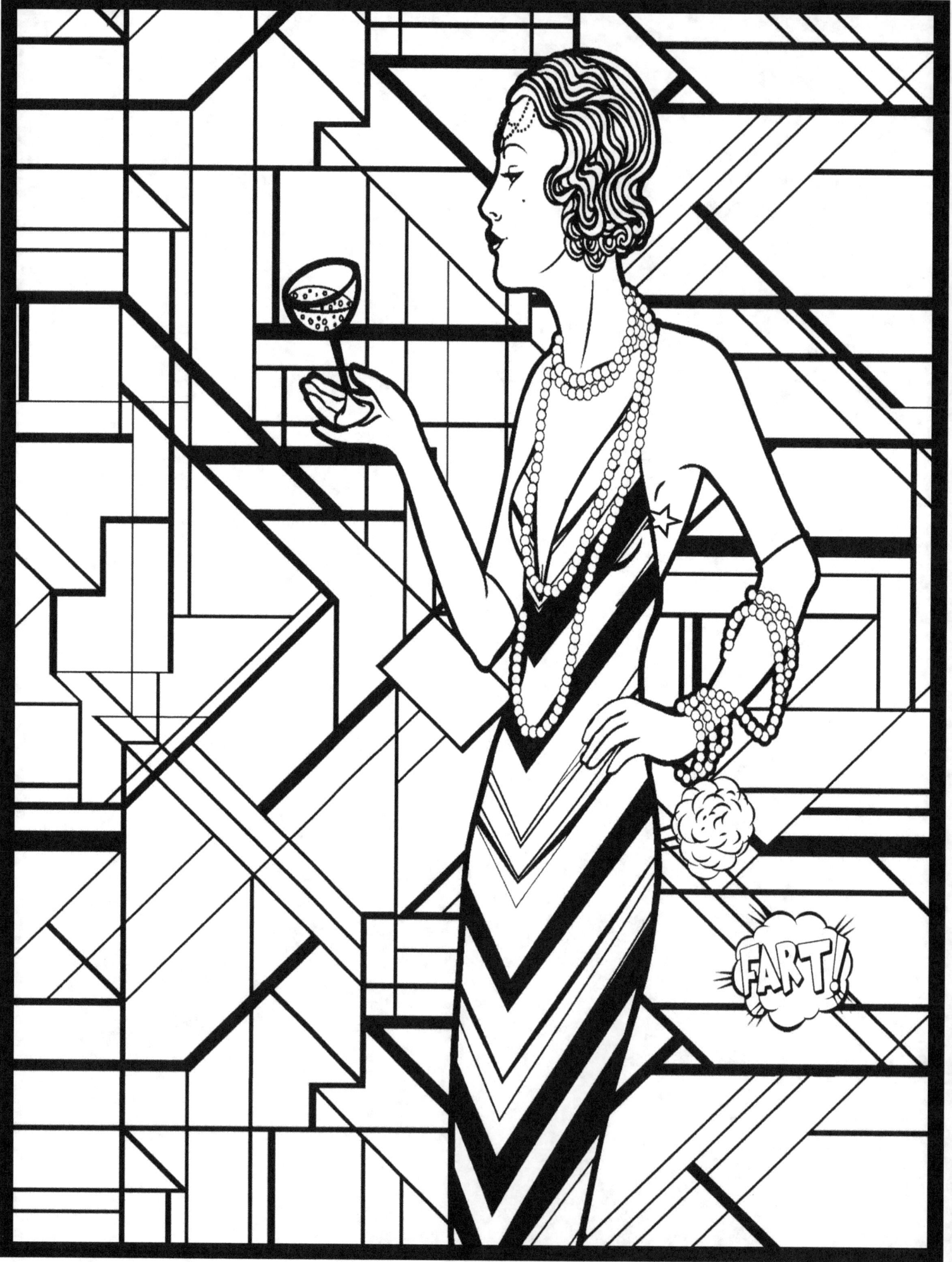

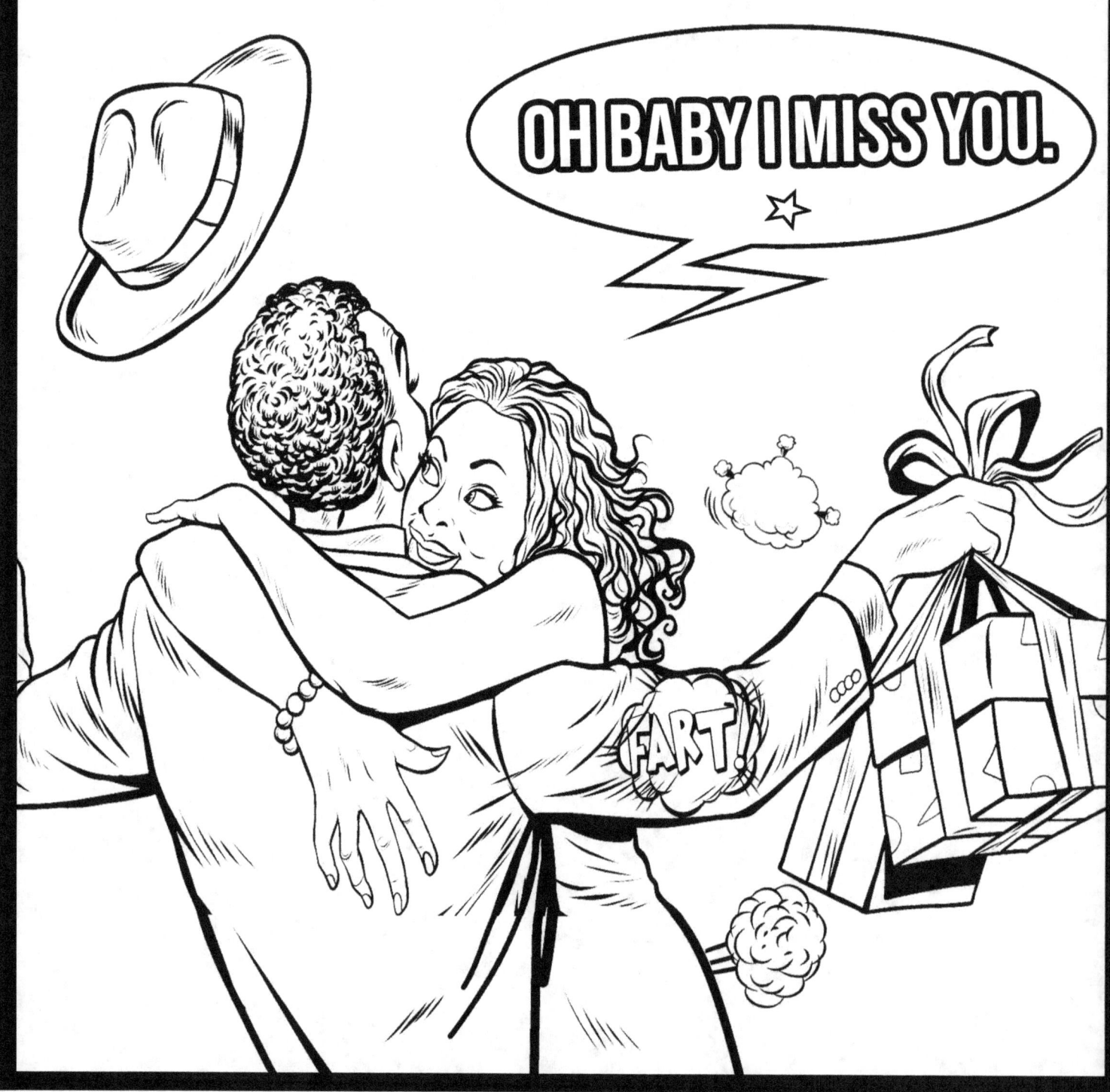

Dear Coloring lover,

Thank you for your recent purchase. We hope you love It. If you do, would you consider posting an online review ? This helps us to continue providing great products, and helps potential buyers to make confident decisions.

Thank you in advance for your review and for being a preferred customer.

We will be forever grateful. Thank you in advance for helping us out!

www.ingramcontent.com/pod-product-compliance
Lightning Source LLC
Chambersburg PA
CBHW080534220526
45465CB00006B/2705